*BUILDING A NATION*

# A MODERN NATION
## 1880-1990

**Written by:**
**Stuart A. Kallen**

1

A MODERN NATION

Published by Abdo & Daughters, 6535 Cecilia Circle, Edina, Minnesota 55439

Library bound edition distributed by Rockbottom Books, Pentagon Tower, P.O. Box 36036, Minneapolis, Minnesota 55435

Library of Congress Number: 90-082629          ISBN: 0-939179-91-1

Cover Illustrations by: Marlene Kallen
Inside Photos by:  AP Wide World Photos, Bettmann Archieves, and
                   Globe Photo.

Cover Illustrations by: Marlene Kallen
**Edited by: Rosemary Wallner**

# TABLE OF CONTENTS

# CHAPTER 1
# THE AGE OF INVENTIONS

## The Industrial Revolution

Cameras! Telephones! Phonographs! Electric Lights! Skyscrapers! Automobiles! Movies! Between 1880 and 1900 all of these inventions and more transformed life in the United States. Thousands of people left their farms and moved to cities to work in the factories. Almost overnight, elevated trains and electrical wires crisscrossed the skies above cities. The peaceful clip-clop of horses' hooves was replaced by the noisy, smokey automobile.

The Industrial Revolution was an age of inventors. Thomas Edison invented the phonograph in 1888. He also invented the electric light, the microphone, the battery, the motion picture and more. Edison said he tried to invent, "one small invention every ten days and one big one every six months."

Other inventors included Alexander Graham Bell, who invented the telephone in 1875. George Eastman invented the portable camera in 1884. In 1890, the modern bicycle was invented. By 1893, over a million Americans were riding bicycles. In 1893, Henry Ford built his first automobile. In 1901, Wilbur and Orville Wright, two bicycle mechanics, flew the first airplane. By 1912, a Model T Ford cost 400 dollars and millions of Americans were buying them. A new society was being built based on machines and mass production. But this new way of living came with a price for people.

*Thomas Edison is shown here after five days and five nights of work to perfect his favorite invention, the phonograph.*

## The Robber Barons

The mass production of thousands of new inventions required steel, oil, minerals and lumber. Many industrial methods were wasteful. Vast areas of land were laid to waste. Hillsides were stripped of their trees. Oil polluted rivers and lakes. Smoke from steel mills blackened the skies over many cities.

A few millionaires like John D. Rockefeller, Andrew Carnegie, Jay Gould, Cornelius Vanderbilt, and J. P. Morgan controlled almost every large company in the United States. Because they were sometimes dishonest in their business dealings, they were known as *robber barons*. The robber barons drove small companies out of business and treated workers badly.

Between 1873 and 1900, five major economic depressions crippled the United States. Many of these depressions were caused in part by the business practices of the robber barons. While some of the robber barons were getting richer, millions of Americans were suffering hardships like unemployment, starvation and homelessness.

Some of the wealthy businessmen used their money to help the people of the United States. Andrew Carnegie, who owned U.S. Steel, spent the last thirty-eight years of his life donating over 350 million dollars. He gave 60 million dollars to cities to build libraries. His other gifts included museums, concert halls and schools.

## America's New Faces
The new factories in the United States needed one important part to make them run: people. Without workers, there would have been no steel, electric lights, or cars. In the early days of the industrial revolution, workers were in short supply. Many companies advertised for workers in Europe. Millions of men, women and children answered the call. The people who left their homelands and came to the United States were called *immigrants*. Most of the immigrants who came to the United States at the turn of the century were Polish, Hungarian, Jewish, Italian, Russian, Greek and Chinese. Many of these people came to the United States to escape prejudice and injustice in their homelands.

Between 1865 and 1930, over 30 million immigrants came to the United States. Many of the new immigrants moved to New York City. As a result, that city grew from 850,000 in 1860 to over 4 million in 1914. Almost every large city in the United States was overcrowded and dirty. Disease and crime were widespread. Sewers, water systems and roads were overworked.

*Immigrants boarding a boat bound for New York City.*

Life was very difficult for the immigrants. Most of them did not speak English. Starting pay in a factory in 1900 was seventy-five cents for a fourteen-hour day. People in the garment industry made eight cents an hour. The labor force included almost two million children under age sixteen. Children, too, worked fourteen hours a day, six days a week. Some children were abandoned because their parents could not care for them.

Factory work was often dangerous. In 1904, over 27,000 workers were killed on the job. Some workers tried to organize labor unions to help them gain better working conditions. But company guards beat or murdered many of the people who tried to organize unions.

Immigrants usually had to live in tiny apartments called *tenements*. Many times, several families lived in one apartment. One New York social worker counted 1,231 people living in only 120 rooms. Another social worker was unable to find a single bathtub in three city blocks of tenements.

Some immigrants did well in the United States. Schools and libraries were available for free. Some schools were open at night so that immigrants could learn to speak English. The Red Cross and the Salvation Army were started to help the poor. President Theodore Roosevelt passed reforms to stop some of the practices of the robber barons. The United States struggled to deal with the millions of new citizens in a newly industrialized society. But changes were taking place in other parts of the world that would challenge the United States' ideals.

## CHAPTER 2
## BECOMING A WORLD POWER

**The Spanish American War**
By 1890, the United States was settled from the East Coast to the West. The days of free land for homesteaders was gone. Many Americans were looking for new lands to conquer and new places to find resources and sell products. Modern ships made travel over the oceans easy and the United States looked to nearby countries to expand its ever growing empire.

William McKinley was elected the twenty-fifth president of the United States in 1896. McKinley believed the United States could expand its rule over any country it wanted to. Many businesses and newspapers also wanted the United States to take over other countries. In 1898, McKinley ordered the *Maine*, an American warship, into a Cuban harbor. Someone, no one knows who, blew up the *Maine* killing the 263 sailors on board. McKinley used the attack as an excuse to start a war with Spain, the country that governed Cuba.

The Spanish had ruled the island of Cuba for 400 years. Another Spanish territory in the Atlantic Ocean was Puerto Rico. Spain also ruled the islands of Guam and the Philippines in the Pacific Ocean.

An unprepared American army invaded the Philippines and Cuba in 1898. The army's rallying cry was, "Remember the *Maine*!" By outnumbering the Spaniards, the Americans won easily. By August 1898, Spain surrendered. The United States bought Cuba, Guam, the West Indies, Puerto Rico and the Philippines from Spain for 20 million dollars.

The people who lived on these islands were angry. They had been fighting for independence from Spain. Now they would have to fight for independence from the United States.

Other countries that the United States invaded in the 1890's were Hawaii in 1893 and Nicaragua in 1894. The United States now governed countries in different parts of the world. The resources and labor in these countries were a benefit to the American economy. At the beginning of the twentieth century, the United States became one of the most powerful countries in the world.

## Trouble in Europe

On June 28, 1914, in the European country of Austria-Hungary, a young man shot and killed the Austrian Archduke Francis Ferdinand and his wife. That one event started a chain reaction that would leave over 20 million people dead, and destroy much of Europe.

After the archduke was assassinated, Austria-Hungary blamed the tiny country of Serbia for the attack. Spurred on by the Germans, Austria-Hungary declared war on Serbia. Russia sided with Serbia and declared war on Germany.

France also supported Serbia so Germany declared war on France on August 3, 1914.

The Germans, expecting a swift victory, wanted to invade France and Russia. Belgium, a neutral country, was in between Germany and France. Germany wanted to march through Belgium to invade France. The German government offered to pay King Albert of Belgium for any damages that would happen to his country. King Albert refused saying, "Belgium is a nation, not a road."

On August 5, 1914, Germany invaded Belgium. England sided with Belgium and declared war on Germany. Within weeks, Turkey sided with Germany, Austria-Hungary and Bulgaria. These countries were known as the Central Alliance. Japan sided with England, France, Russia, Greece, Romania and Portugal. These countries were known as the Allies.

By the end of 1914, both sides had dug miles of trenches on the eastern and western battlefronts. Soldiers fired on each other from the trenches. Thousands of soldiers died while their armies moved ahead a few inches at a time. In spite of the thousands of deaths, most people expected the war to be over soon.

## The United States Reacts

Europe had not had a major war since 1815. When war broke out in the summer of 1914, the United States was shocked. The conflict started in one week and quickly became incredibly violent. In 1915 alone, over 1.5 million French, 313,000 English and 850,000 Germans died. Modern technology was used to help the armies slaughter each other. World War I was the first war to use long-range missles, machine guns, airplanes, tanks, submarines and poison gases.

America's twenty-eighth president, Woodrow Wilson, did not want to choose sides in the war. He wanted the United States to remain neutral. Most Americans, however, chose sides with the Allies. Wilson's attitude began to change in 1915.

## The United States Tries to Remain Neutral

The Germans had been patrolling the North Sea in submarines for several months. They were trying to keep supply ships from entering English harbors. The Germans tried to sink any ship they saw in the North Sea. On May 7, 1915, a German submarine sank the *Lusitania* a British passenger ship. Among the 1,200 people who died, 128 were Americans. Germany did not want a war with the

United States, so the government apologized for sinking the ship. But the German submarine attacks continued.

Woodrow Wilson tried several times, without success, to convince Germany to end the war. In 1916, Wilson doubled the size of the U.S. Army and started to build hundreds of warships. In March 1917, Wilson discovered that the Germans were trying to get Mexico to attack the United States. On April 6, 1917, the United States declared war on Germany. Soon, Americans were being sent to Europe to fight in the bloody World War.

*Soldiers fighting in World War I*

## The Yanks Are Coming

Americans were eager to help the Allies. The Allies were suffering huge losses and only the Americans could save them. In one battle alone the English suffered 420,000 casualties. In the Battle of Verdun the French had lost over 460,000 men.

However, in April 1917, the United States only had 200,000 soldiers in the Army. But because of the draft and voluntary enlistments, by November 1918, the United States Army had over 5 million soldiers.

Most American troops did not arrive in Europe until 1918. When the Americans did arrive, things looked bad for the Allies. The Germans were within fifty miles of Paris. With the fresh American soldiers, the French drove the Germans out of France. By sheer numbers of men, the Americans forced the Germans to surrender on November 11, 1918, eleven months after they had landed in Europe.

World War I was over. The number of people killed on each side was astounding: France —over 6 million; England — over 3 million; Germany — over 7 million; the United States —over 350,000. Europe was in ruins. People called World War I "the war to end all wars."

# CHAPTER 3
# GOOD TIMES, BAD TIMES

## Electricity and Cars

Before World War I, only 20 percent of Americans had electricity. By 1929, over 70 percent had electricity. Now, most Americans could enjoy radios, electric refrigerators, vacuum cleaners, washing machines and sewing machines.

Housework was made easier by these electrical appliances. American women now had more free time. Women were allowed to vote for the first time in 1919. Many women stopped wearing long dresses and bulky clothing. Some women cut their hair short, wore short skirts and makeup and danced the Charleston. They were called *flappers*. Many women were feeling a degree of freedom and equality for the first time.

The automobile was quickly changing the country. By 1924, a Model T Ford cost only 240 dollars. Between 1920 and 1929, the number of cars in the United States jumped from 8 million to 24 million. By 1929, one out of nine workers had a job related to the auto industry. Over 121,000 gas stations operated in the United States. A whole new way of life sprang up around drive-ins, billboards, motels, traffic lights, traffic jams and honking horns. By 1929, Americans had spent over 30 billion dollars on cars.

*Henry Ford seated in one of his automobiles made in the early 1900's.*

## Prohibition

In 1919, Congress passed the 18th Amendment to the Constitution making it illegal to buy, sell, or drink alcohol. Because the law prohibited people from drinking, it was called *Prohibition*.

An entire illegal industry sprang up to fill the demand for whiskey, beer and wine. Bootleggers, moonshiners, racketeers, crooked politicians, corrupt policemen and just plain folks, worked together to deliver illegal alcohol to the public. Clubs, called *speakeasies*, opened in basements and back rooms to serve drinks. By 1933, over 121,000 speakeasies operated in the United States.

Gangsters, like Al Capone, made millions by selling illegal alcohol. His gangs delivered up to 70 million gallons of alcohol to Americans every year. Gangs fought each other for turf. Police and F.B.I. agents could only arrest a small percentage of the people breaking the law. When Prohibition ended in 1933, the gangs that had made millions from bootlegging put their money into other legal and illegal businesses.

## The Roaring Twenties

By the 1920's, two new inventions, movies and radio, occupied many people's free time. In 1929, theaters sold 110 million tickets in a country of 122 million people. The new American hero's were movie stars.

The radio also became very popular. For the first time, people could listen to sports, news and stories in their own homes.

People had more time for sports and the radio delivered them. Baseball, football, boxing and basketball games attracted millions of new fans. For the first time, fans could follow the careers of sports heroes like boxing's Jack Dempsey and baseball's Babe Ruth. Sports arenas sprang up everywhere as cities formed their own teams.

Jazz music, usually played by black people, became more popular in the twenties. Suddenly, white people were paying attention to black culture. The Harlem area of New York City, where many blacks lived, enjoyed an era of flowering creativity. Black people took to the streets to protest prejudice. Black poets, authors, and musicians wrote about black pride. In other areas of the country, however, terrorist groups like the Ku Klux Klan were becoming stronger.

The Klan beat and murdered innocent black people.

Life seemed free and easy in the twenties and the decade had many nicknames: the Jazz Age, the Roaring Twenties, the Flapper Era, the Golden Twenties. But the good times were about to come to a crashing halt.

## The Crash

The Roaring Twenties were fueled by new inventions and Prohibition. But people needed money to buy cars, radios and bootleg liquor. Everybody was trying to get rich quick. During the Roaring Twenties, people made fortunes overnight in the stock market. Newspapers and radios made it seem like anyone could make a million dollars overnight buying and selling stocks. During the twenties, many people borrowed money from banks to buy things they could not afford. People also borrowed money to invest in get-rich-quick schemes. For a few years, some people did get rich. But farmers and working people had a hard time making ends meet.

On Thursday, October 24, 1929, the stock market crashed. Thousands of people lost millions of dollars as the prices of stocks they owned went plummeting down. Most stocks had been bought by people who had borrowed money from banks. When the prices of the stocks fell, people could not pay their bank loans and the banks closed. When the banks closed, people lost their life's savings. Suddenly, people could not afford to buy radios and cars and washing machines, so the factories closed. When the factories closed, thousands of people lost their jobs. When they could not pay the rent, many people were forced to live on the street. Because so many people were unhappy, this period in history is known as the Depression.

## The Depression

By 1932, Americans' spirits had reached an all-time low. One out of every four people was unemployed. Two thousand banks had closed. Auto sales were down 80 percent. People were living in cardboard shanty towns called *Hoovervilles*, named after President Herbert Hoover. A madman named Adolf Hitler had gained power in Germany and was threatening to lead Europe into another world war.

To make matters worse, there was a drought in the Midwest. Desperately needed food was dying in the fields for lack of rain. Hordes of grasshoppers invaded and destroyed what was left of the crops. From North Dakota to Oklahoma to Texas, the dry, powdery topsoil blew off the land. The skies were blackened by the blowing dirt. As far east as Cleveland, Ohio, people had to cover their faces to protect themselves from the dust. People began to call the Midwest the Dustbowl. Farmers were thrown off of their farms when they could not pay their bank loans.

Mental hospitals filled up. People who had been millionaires a few years before were now begging on street corners. Ruined businessmen killed themselves by jumping out of windows. The United States was at a standstill.

## The New Deal

In 1932, Franklin Delano Roosevelt (FDR) was elected the thirty-second president. Roosevelt promised Americans a "New Deal." He wanted to get the country back to work. In 1933, he brought thousands of young people to Washington, D.C., to help solve the problems of the Depression. During his first 100 days in office, Roosevelt passed fifteen laws. The laws started programs to help the poor and the unemployed.

The Civilian Conservation Corps (CCC) was started to employ men between the ages of eighteen and twenty-five. These men planted trees and built roads in parks like Yosemite in California and Yellowstone in Wyoming. Roosevelt also started programs to help banks, industries, and farmers. Social Security was started to help the elderly. The Tennessee Valley Authority (TVA) was started to build dams that would bring electricity to farmers.

In 1936, the Works Progress Administration (WPA) put 3 million people to work building over 2,500 hospitals, 5,000 schools, 13,000 parks and playgrounds and 1,000 airports. The WPA also paid artists to paint murals on buildings. The group hired photographers and writers to record the Depression's effects on the country. They hired actors and entertainers to stage shows. The WPA also helped students work their way through college. Unfortunately, the WPA could not help everyone. Most people were living on monthly government checks called *Relief*.

## The Dirty Thirties

Although FDR's programs were helping some people, the economy improved only a little. In 1937, Roosevelt tried to cut the new programs and let the United States stand on its own. The Supreme Court ruled some programs unconstitutional. Many businessmen thought Roosevelt's programs resembled communism. By 1938, FDR could not pass one law through Congress to help hungry Americans.

Without the government's help, the economy plunged even further than it had in 1930. Unemployment increased by 4 million in seven months. One-sixth of New York City was on Relief. One-third of Americans were poorly housed, fed and clothed. Although many of FDR's agencies still function in the government today, by

1938, Roosevelt's New Deal was at an end. But events were happening in Europe that would end the Depression with a bang.

*Franklin Delano Roosevelt (FDR) 32nd. President of the United States.*

# CHAPTER 4
# MARCHING INTO WORLD WAR II

## The Devil in Germany

During the 1930's most Americans did not pay attention to events in other countries. They were worried about finding work, housing and food. But the Depression that affected the United States also affected European countries. After World War I, Germany was forced to pay other countries for the damages it had done. This caused the German economy to collapse. German money became worthless. People had to load wheelbarrows full of German money just to buy a few groceries. Desperate people starved in the streets of this once powerful nation.

In 1932, the frustrated German people elected Adolf Hitler to lead Germany. Hitler was the leader of the Nazi Party. He promised to rebuild Germany. He also promised to regain the lands that Germany had lost in World War I. Hitler told the Germans that Jewish people had caused Germany to lose the war. He said that the Jews were causing all of Germany's problems. Although this was an outrageous lie, many people believed him.

In 1933, Hitler made himself dictator of Germany. He killed all his opposition and started a program to kill all Jewish people. He built concentration camps where people were sent to work like slaves until they died. At the concentration camps, the Nazis built huge gas chambers and ovens. People were rounded up by the millions and killed in the gas chambers. After they were dead, their bodies were burned in the ovens.

Huge piles of clothes, shoes and glasses that were taken from the prisoners were kept in warehouses at the camps. People's heads were shaved and huge mounds of hairs were saved. Mad doctors performed horrible experiments on living people. Torture, murder and mass killing became a way of life for the Nazis.

In 1939, Hitler invaded Poland. There, his soldiers rounded up Jewish people, Gypsies, disabled people and anyone who opposed him. The people were sent to concentration camps to be killed. By the end of World War II, Hitler had killed 12 million people in the camps. One-third of the Jews in Europe — 6 million people — were murdered. This era is known as the Holocaust. The word means a large, terrible destruction. Hitler and his men committed some of the most horrible crimes against humanity ever recorded in human history.

## World War II Begins

In the 1930's, the United States did not know of Hitler's plan for Europe and the Jews. Other dictators were causing trouble elsewhere. The Italian dictator Benito Mussolini had controlled his country since 1922. His followers were known as Facists. Italy invaded Africa in 1935. In Japan, Emperor Hirohito ordered the invasion of China in 1931. In 1936, Italy, Germany and Japan formed an alliance known as the Axis Powers.

*Italian Dictator Benito Mussolini (left) and Adolf Hitler.*

On September 1, 1939, Germany's army invaded Poland. Entire villages were laid to waste. Polish townspeople were lined up against walls and killed by German machine guns. Two days later, England and France declared war on Germany. The United States remained neutral, although most Americans supported the Allies.

By June 22, 1940, German soldiers had taken over Denmark, Norway, Belgium and France. By August, they were bombing England. The Nazis fought a new kind of war called the *Blitzkrieg*. Rows of swift moving tanks and armored trucks would roll into a country while airplanes bombed its cities. Within hours, the country would fall to the Nazis. In each country Hitler invaded, the Jewish people who lived there were packed into boxcars on trains and taken to concentration camps to be slaughtered.

**The United States Declares War**
On December 7, 1941, the roaring planes of the Japanese air force broke the Sunday morning calm at the American naval base in Pearl Harbor, Hawaii. The planes dropped bombs and within

thirty minutes 3,700 American soldiers were killed. Over one thousand were wounded. Fifteen battleships and 150 airplanes were destroyed in the surprise attack. The next day, the grim and shaken Franklin Roosevelt, who had just been elected president for the third time, declared war on Japan. Several days later, Germany and Italy declared war on the United States.

Almost everyone in the United States pitched in on the war effort. Industries that were idle during the Depression started to produce again. Six million men and women joined the armed forces. Ten million men were drafted. Women started to work in factories. Roosevelt set production goals for 1942. He wanted 60,000 airplanes, 45,000 tanks, and 20,000 antiaircraft guns. Those goals were met. In 1943 and 1944, U.S. factories exceeded that goal. The United States produced more war supplies than Germany, Italy and Japan combined. The Depression was over and the war was on.

## The Fight

Almost every country in the world chose sides in
World War II. Forty-nine nations sided with the
Allies. Only nine fought for the Axis. World War II
was actually two separate wars fought over a
huge area of the world. The United States,
England, Australia and New Zealand fought Japan
from Alaska to Java (in Indonesia) and from
Hawaii to India. This was called the war in the
Pacific. The other front pitted the Axis against the
Allies in Europe and Africa.

Several years passed as the war reaped its bloody
harvest of death and destruction all over the
world. In the United States, Roosevelt was elected
to his fourth term as president. Roosevelt was the
only president in American history to be elected
four times. (After the war, Congress changed the
law so that a president could only serve two
terms.)

In 1944, over 3 million Allied troops gathered in
England. They prepared to invade the Germans in
France. On June 6, 1944, the largest land, sea and
air invasion in history began. 130,000 soldiers
crawled onto the beaches in Normandy, France,
into the face of heavy German gunfire. Thousands
died, but within six weeks, France was free of

German rule. During the winter of 1944-45, American General Dwight D. Eisenhower's troops recaptured most of Europe from the Nazis.

By the spring of 1945, the German war machine was in ruins. The Russians pushed in from the east while the Americans attacked on the west. On April 12, President Roosevelt died. Vice-President Harry S. Truman became America's president. On April 30, Adolf Hitler committed suicide in his bunker in Berlin while Russian guns pounded the city. On May 7, 1945, Germany surrendered. The war in Europe was over.

## Nuclear Destruction

Although Germany was defeated, the war in the Pacific raged on. The Allies faced heavy casualties in hard won battles on the islands of Okinawa and Iwo Jima. Japan did not seem like it was about to surrender. President Truman estimated that 500,000 soldiers would die if the United States attacked Japan. So Truman decided to use a new secret weapon to end the war: the atomic bomb.

On August 6, 1945, the United States dropped an atomic bomb on Hiroshima, Japan. The force was the same as 20,000 tons of dynamite. The temperature near the center of the bombsight was

1 million degrees. Buildings and people vanished in the explosion and the city was totally flattened. People who were miles away were burned all over their bodies. Radiation given off by the bomb killed people for years afterward. On August 9, another atom bomb was dropped on Nagasaki. The two explosions killed 150,000 Japanese men, women and children. On August 14, 1945, Japan surrendered. World War II was over.

## The World Changes

Fifty-five million people died in World War II, including 30 million Russians. Over 290,000 Americans died and 390,000 were wounded. Europe was in ruins. Russia and the United States were now the most powerful countries in the world.

When the mushroom cloud exploded over Hiroshima, the nuclear age was born.

When the United States was the only country to have nuclear bombs, Americans felt safe. They thought that atom bombs would never have to be used. But as the 1950's dawned, new events challenged that way of thinking.

*U.S. Marines try and clean up beach after heavy bombardment in South Pacific Ocean.*

# CHAPTER 5
# THE POST WAR WORLD

## The Cold War

In 1945, the Allies agreed to let the freed
European countries elect their own officials. From
the start, Russia ignored the agreement. Instead,
Russia set up Communist dictatorships in Poland,
Hungary, Romania, Bulgaria, Albania,
Czechoslovakia and East Germany. Russia's
leader, Joseph Stalin, ran these countries much
like Hitler had. Murder and assassination were
used to keep people under strict control. In 1949,
Russians exploded their own atomic bomb. At the
same time, another Communist, Mao Tse-tung,
took control of China. Americans were shocked
and afraid that the Communists were going to
take over the entire world.

President Truman ordered development of an
even larger nuclear bomb, the hydrogen bomb.
He also started to rebuild the U.S. Army. Soon,
Russia and the United States were racing to build
more powerful bombs and larger armies. This was
the beginning of the arms race. Because there
was no war but countries were preparing for one,

this era is called the Cold War. Distrust and fear kept the United States and Russia from making any attempts at peace.

In 1950, only five years after World War II had ended, Americans were at war with the Communists for control of Korea. By the time that war was over in 1953, over 56,000 Americans had died.

The threat of Communists taking over the United States was hard to prove. Many people, however, believed that the United States was full of spies who wanted the Russians to take over the country. American actors, artists, musicians, writers and politicians were called into Congress to swear their loyalty to the United States. The Constitution protects people from having to make such claims. But many people's careers were ruined if they refused this request.


## The Fifties

After the war, the United States became the wealthiest nation in the world. General Dwight D. Eisenhower was elected thirty-fourth president in 1952. Ex-soldiers got married, built homes, bought cars and started families. Millions of babies were born after the war, and many of them became teenagers in the fifties. This generation is called the *baby boomers*. In the fifties, teenagers listened to rock and roll music for the first time. Televisions appeared in every household. Americans enjoyed their prosperity for the rest of the decade.

## The Kennedy Years

As the 1960's began, the United States was becoming a younger nation. The average age of Americans dipped below thirty years old. This was reflected in the election of John Fitzgerald Kennedy as thirty-fifth president in 1960. Kennedy was only forty-three years old, the youngest president ever elected. Kennedy led the country through several years of economic, social and scientific progress.

The United States launched its first manned space flight on February 20, 1962. Astronaut John Glenn circled Earth three times and then returned. Americans cheered as their country entered the space age. Kennedy promised to put a man on the moon by 1970. In July 1969, Neil Armstrong became the first man to walk on the moon.

*John Fitzgerald Kennedy (right). The youngest president elected, talking with his younger brother Bobby then Attourney General.*

Kennedy and other Americans pushed hard for civil rights reforms. On August 28, 1963, over 300,000 black people gathered near the Lincoln Memorial in Washington, D.C., to protest for civil rights. Dr. Martin Luther King, Jr., addressed the crowd.

The sixties were a time of much racial unrest. Black people took to the streets again and again to demand equal rights. By the end of the decade, reforms were put into place to help blacks obtain equal rights.

*Dr. Martin Luther King, Jr. Civil Rights Leader.*

On November 22, 1963, John F. Kennedy was gunned down on the streets of Dallas, Texas. Americans sat stunned through a bleak Thanksgiving as Kennedy was buried in Arlington, Virginia. The innocence of the eary 1960's faded away as Lyndon Baines Johnson was sworn in as the next president.

## Vietnam

Vietnam is a country in Southeast Asia. During the fifties, the country was divided in half because of a civil war. Russia, now called the Soviet Union, started supplying North Vietnam with weapons. The United States government was afraid that another country would fall to communism. The U.S. government started supplying South Vietnam with weapons and advisers. In 1963, 16,000 Americans were in Vietnam. The North Vietnamese were ferocious fighters. Over 150,000 South Vietnamese soldiers could not stop 15,000 North Vietnamese who were known as Vietcong.

In 1965, Johnson ordered 20,000 troops to Vietnam. By the end of 1968, over 536,000 Americans were fighting in Vietnam. Twenty

*United States soldiers wade through muddy water in Vietnam.*

thousand had died. In three years, the United States dropped more bombs on the tiny country of North Vietnam than they dropped in all of World War II.

## The Sixties

After Kennedy's assassination, the United States needed something to cheer it up. A group of musicians from England, called the Beatles, provided that cheer. In February 1964, the Beatles landed in New York for their first American tour. Thousands of fans were at the airport screaming for their heroes. People bought millions of Beatle records throughout the sixties. The Beatles revolutionized music and fashions. The Beatles sang about world peace and other important issues. Experimental rock and roll became the sound of the sixties.

In San Francisco, thousands of people calling themselves hippies demonstrated for peace and love for all people. Psychedelic rock and roll, love-ins, long hair and Flower Power swept the country from east to west. Along with the call for peace, hippies and other Americans demanded women's equal rights and protection of the environment.

*Television personality Ed Sullivan welcomes the Beatles to America.*

## Vietnam Protests

Millions of baby boomers reached draft age as the
war in Vietnam careened out of control. Many
Americans did not believe in the war. Protests
broke out in cities all over the United States.
Police used tear gas and billy clubs to break up
protests.

Richard Nixon was elected president in 1968. Nixon promised to end the war, but instead he increased it by invading Cambodia, Vietnam's neighbor, in 1970. When thousands of people protested this action at Kent State College in Ohio, the National Guard was called in. On May 4, 1970, the National Guard opened fire on the crowd, killing four students and injuring nine. People were outraged.

On May 9, over 200,000 people gathered in Washington to protest the war. Nixon finally pulled many of the troops out of Vietnam in 1973. Over 56,000 Americans died in Vietnam, and countless others were permanently disabled. Thousands of Americans were taken prisoner. Because of the war the entire area of Southeast Asia suffered greatly.

## Nixon's Fall
In 1971, Congress lowered the voting age from twenty-one to eighteen. Republican president Richard Nixon was reelected in 1972. During

*A body of a student shot by national Guardsmen during a Vietnam War protest at Kent State University.*

Nixon's campaign, some of his advisers ordered a break-in at the Democratic Party's headquarters in the Watergate office building in Washington, D.C. His advisers wanted to steal documents from the Democrats to help Nixon win the presidency. After Nixon was reelected, the press found out about the break-in at Watergate. One by one, Nixon's advisers were put on trial, found guilty and sent to prison. Attorney General John Mitchell was forced to resign from office. Evidence showed that Nixon tried to cover up the break-in and thwart the FBI's investigation of it.

The Watergate Hearings before Congress were televised and millions of Americans watched. Americans were stunned when they heard the secret plans of Nixon and his advisers. Congress was ready to impeach Nixon. Finally, on August 8, 1974, Richard Nixon became the first president to ever resign from office. Vice-President Gerald Ford took over as president.

## The Seventies

Jimmy Carter was elected president in 1976. During his term, the country of Iran was in the middle of a revolution. The United States depended on Iran and other countries in the Mideast for oil. Almost half of the oil used in the United States came from Mideastern countries. The Organization of Petroleum Exporting Countries (OPEC) decided to raise the price of oil. A barrel of oil cost $1.20 in 1969. In 1978, the price of a barrel of oil soared to $20. This made the price of gasoline in the United States jump from twenty-five cents a gallon to over one dollar a gallon in a few years. When the price of oil rose, the price of everything from a loaf of bread to a new car also rose. This is called *inflation*.

In November 1979, revolutionaries in Iran stormed the American Embassy and took fifty Americans as hostage. Americans watched helplessly as the hostages were paraded, blindfolded, before television cameras. Americans counted the days that the hostages were prisoners in Iran.

## The Eighties

When Republican Ronald Reagan was elected president in 1980, Americans felt that they were not in control of world events. But the hostages were released in 1980 and inflation started to slow.

Reagan's first days in office were busy. For the first time in forty years, Republicans controlled the Senate. Reagan cut taxes and started the largest peacetime military buildup in history. Reagan had to pay for the buildup with borrowed money. Spending money that is borrowed is called *deficit spending*. During Reagans term the national deficit tripled. Now the United States was spending billions of dollars that was being borrowed from foreign countries like Japan and Germany.

In 1984, Reagan was elected to his second term as president. At the beginning of his term, he distrusted the Soviet Union and continued to spend money on the build-up of nuclear arms. But his feelings changed. On December 8, 1987, Reagan and Soviet leader Mikhail Gorbachev agreed to sign the INF Treaty (Intermediate Nuclear Forces). The treaty stated that both

*Ronald Reagan elected president in 1980.*

countries would destroy their intermediate range nuclear missiles. This was the first agreement to rid the world of a whole class of nuclear weapons.

This treaty fulfilled what Reagan had said in his first Inaugural Address. "Peace is the highest aspiration of the American people. We will negotiate for it, sacrifice for it, we will not surrender for it — now or ever."

In the eighties, computers became very popular. Cable TV, personal computers, VCR's, FAX machines and compact disks changed the way Americans lived and worked.

*Reagan served two full terms as America's president.*

## Into the Nineties

In 1988, George Bush was elected the forty-first president of the United States. Bush ran his campaign on the promise of no new taxes.

Bush had been active in the government for many years. He had been the ambassador to China and, from 1973 to 1976, he had run the Central Intelligence Agency (CIA). Bush also served as vice-president under Ronald Reagan from 1980 to 1988.

As president, George Bush pursued global diplomacy. Like Reagan, Bush continued to make contacts with Soviet Union leader Mikhail Gorbachev. Together, Bush and Gorbachev helped to reduce nuclear arms throughout the world.

*George Bush, 41st president of the United States.*

In November 1989, the Berlin Wall tumbled down. The wall had been built in 1961 by Communists to keep people from escaping from the countries they ruled. Europeans rejoiced as the wall that had divided East from West crumbled into dust. Communism was not working, and Mikhail Gorbachev needed Western money to help his country.

The United States had been spending billions of dollars to keep armies and weapons in Germany since World War II. Americans had been afraid that the Soviet Union would try to take over Europe in much the same way that Hitler had done. The Soviet Union and the United States had been pointing nuclear bombs at each other for forty years. With the Soviets loosening their hold on Europe, the threat of war has been reduced greatly. The Cold War seemed to be over.

*Mikhail Gorbachev, president of the Soviet Union.*

With the Cold War threat diminished, many Americans felt that the greatest threat facing them in the nineties was environmental hazards. The automobile and industries that ushered in the twentieth century had polluted the land, air and water. Global warming, the destruction of rain forests and nuclear waste were problems that needed a lot of attention. People realized that what happened in one part of the world affected people thousands of miles away.

Since World War II, the two most powerful nations on the earth, the Soviet Union and the United States, had been spending trillions of dollars to prepare for war. At the beginning of the 1990's peace is broke out all over. People from many countries joined together to solve the world's problems.

## A Final Word

As the story of the United States unfolded it became one of the most unusual and interesting stories in history. In a very short period of time, from Christopher Columbus to George Bush, Americans have changed the face of the Globe and the lives of the people on it. As a new century dawns the United States continues to expand on its experiment of freedom and democracy.

In an ever changing world, no one can say what the future will bring, but it is certain that whatever happens, the United States will remain a powerful country because of the strength and pride of its people.

*George Bush (left), Ronald Reagan (center) and Mikhail Gorbachev in front of the Statue of Liberty in New York.*

# INDEX